Micro Hydro
Electric Power
Ray Holland

T0266280

Practical
ACTION
PUBLISHING

Practical Action Publishing Ltd
25 Albert Street, Rugby, CV21 2SD, Warwickshire, UK
www.practicalactionpublishing.com

© Intermediate Technology Publications 1983

ISBN 13 Paperback: 9781853393631
ISBN Library Ebook: 9781780444154
Book DOI: http://dx.doi.org/10.3362/9781780444154

Since 1974, Practical Action Publishing has published and disseminated
books and information in support of international development work
throughout the world. Practical Action Publishing is a trading name of
Practical Action Publishing Ltd (Company Reg. No. 1159018), the
wholly owned publishing company of Practical Action. Practical Action
Publishing trades only in support of its parent charity objectives and
any profits are covenanted back to Practical Action (Charity Reg. No.
247257, Group VAT Registration No. 880 9924 76).

PREFACE

Over the last few years there has been a growing realization in developing countries that micro hydro-electric power plants have an important role to play in the economic development of remote, particularly mountainous, rural areas. There are many agricultural and other industrial processes that can generate income for rural communities if carried out on a small scale. Micro hydro-electric plants can provide power for such processes more cheaply than alternatives such as diesel generators or extension of high voltage grids and, in addition, provide domestic electricity. However, there is a shortage of technical information on these very small power plants. This paper is intended to provide an introduction to the technical, economic and managerial aspects up to the point of working out how much power could be generated and what type of hardware to choose. ITDG will later be publishing a technical manual on micro hydro engineering and management practice. ITDG can also offer consultancy services for feasibility studies, project design and implementation.

Ray Holland
Rugby, 1983.

Ray Holland is an Electrical Engineer working as Project Manager with the Industrial Services Division of ITDG.

Over the past four years he has been managing micro hydro projects in many developing countries including Sri Lanka, Nepal, Thailand and Colombia.

His objective is to find a model for the successful widespread dissemination of the means to harness this important source of power.

We would like to thank Evans Engineering of Launceston, Cornwall, and Peter Fraenkel of I.T.Power, for permission to reproduce the photographs.

CONTENTS

LIST OF ILLUSTRATIONS

INTRODUCTION

Like all forms of renewable energy, micro hydro-electric power has recently attracted worldwide interest; and yet the basic technology is not new. While seeming to offer power at extremely low annual running cost and with very few technical complications, there are as yet few countries where its use has become widespread. It is found that design, installation and management have all to be treated very carefully. It has been demonstrated in many places that small hydro power can make a very important contribution towards rural development, such as in the Peoples' Republic of China, where some 80,000 mini hydro plants have been installed over the last twenty years. But there are pitfalls for the unwary. This paper gives an introduction to the techniques and a guide how to approach mini hydro projects. It is concerned only with systems of up to approximately 100kW output.

3kW Pelton Wheel with Electronic Control.

BACKGROUND

Water power was used for hundreds of years throughout Asia, Europe and parts of Africa to drive a variety of industrial machinery, from grain mills through forge bellows and trip hammers to pumps and textile mills. The fall of running water was converted to mechanical shaft power by a water wheel with either a vertical shaft (the oldest) or horizontal shaft. All these water-wheels used only a low head of water up to a maximum of 6 or 7 metres. Their chief limitation for driving machinery was their low rotational speed.

The modern water turbines invented in the nineteenth century gave much higher speeds and allowed the use of higher heads of water and thus the extraction of greater potential energy from the same quantity of water. With the invention of electrical generators the energy could be transmitted more efficiently and distributed more widely to where it was wanted. Hydro plants have been built all over the world. Huge, highly capital-intensive schemes have been constructed to feed extensive (and expensive) grid systems supplying power to large energy-intensive industries such as aluminium smelting and to urban areas.

The best geographical areas for exploiting small-scale hydro power are those where there are steep rivers flowing all year round such as the hill areas of countries with high year-round rainfall or the great mountain ranges and their foothills, e.g. the Andes chain, the Himalayas, or islands with moist marine climates, such as the Caribbean islands, the Philippines and Indonesia.

Small-scale hydro power in these areas represents an economic alternative to distributing centralised power through high voltage grids, particularly for isolated rural communities. In hilly rural areas grid electricity from large centralised power stations is inevitably an expensive utility to provide and cannot pay for itself unless there is a high guaranteed demand. Power from diesel generators is more

1

expensive to provide than hydro because of the high running costs (see Appendix II). The most valuable use to which small-scale hydro can currently be put is powering small local industries, the majority of which will probably be agriculturally based, to substitute for commercial fuel and to raise the income earning potential of the local community by processing local products. A hydro plant installed for such a purpose can provide domestic power as a by-product but the heat power demand for cooking is often too high for the available electrical supply from a micro hydro plant and it is then necessary to use techniques such as heat storage cookers of low power input. (Design information available from ITDG.)

In some areas water-wheels may still be a viable technology, particularly where manufacture of turbines is not feasible. However, this paper is concerned purely with turbines.

Fig. 1 shows a typical micro hydro installation, where water from a river is diverted into a canal to gain head before running down through the penstock pipe to the turbine.

Water into Watts

To determine the power potential of the water flowing in a river or stream it is necessary to determine both the flow rate of the water and the head through which the water can be made to fall.

The **flow rate** is the quantity of water usually measured in cubic feet or litres flowing past a point in a given time. Typical flow rate units are cubic feet per second (cusecs) or litres per second.

The **head** is the vertical height in feet or metres from the turbine up to the point where the water enters the intake pipe (or penstock). (In the case of reaction turbines (see below) it may also include the suction head of the draft tube below the turbine down to the tail race water level.)

For methods of measuring flow rate and head see Appendix IV.

Turbines convert the potential energy of water at a height

2

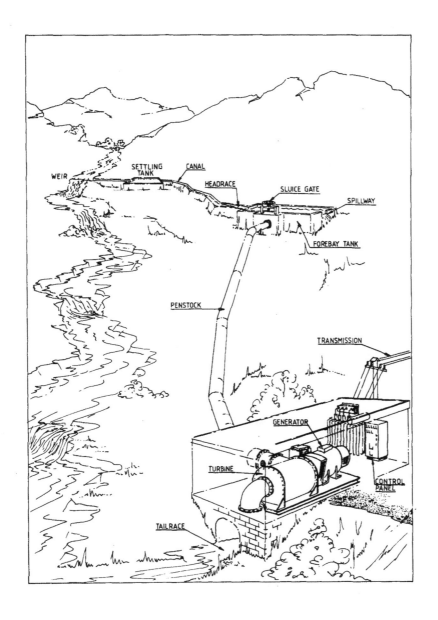

FIGURE 1

of 'h' meters into shaft energy dependent on the flow rate of water and the efficiency of conversion so that with 'Q' litres per second flowing through the turbine per second from a head 'h' the power produced is: **k.Q.h (kilowatts)**. Values of k for Q and h in different units are shown in the attached table.

UNITS		
Q	h	k
cu. ft/s	ft.	.05
litres/s	metres	.006

Where the overall conversion efficiency (generator and turbine losses combined) is taken to be 60%.

$$\frac{80}{100} \times \frac{75}{100} = \frac{60}{100}$$

(The efficiency of a small turbine is typically 75% and and generator efficiency 80%).

Example: A turbine generator set operating on a head of 10 metres with a flow of 300 litres per second will deliver approximately (.006 x 300 x 10) = 18 kilowatts of electricity.

This energy would otherwise be dissipated in spray and in vortices and ultimately in a fractional increase in temperature of the water.

Figure 2 shows the power produced by various heads and flow rates assuming an overall efficiency of 60%. It also shows the heads which are suitable for the three types of turbine.

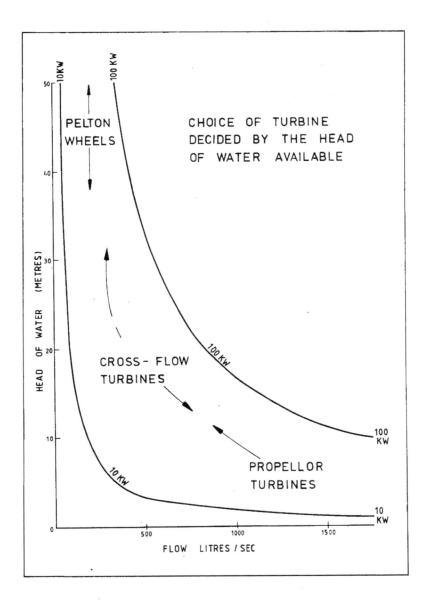

FIGURE 2

HYDROLOGY

When planning a micro hydro plant or a number of plants for a particular area it is essential to have a good estimate of the seasonal and year-to-year variations in river flow that can be expected. Ideally this would be done by recording the variations in the water flow over a whole year and then comparing that year's daily rainfall figures with the records from previous years. In practice such an approach is rarely possible. The best alternative is to work out the catchment area for the river up to the point of diversion. This can be done from large-scale maps or by surveying.

An estimate of the flow duration curve for the site can then be made by comparing records from gauged rivers in the area. The rainfall: run-off characteristic should be very similar provided that the predominant soil types are similar. Rainfall data from the site can then be used to calculate the flow duration curve. If no rainfall data is available from the site itself then rainfall will have to be estimated by adjustment of figures from the nearest, most appropriate rain gauge station. Iso-hyetal maps of rainfall distribution may also be available for the region. Of course the flow prediction must be checked by spot readings of river flow or preferably from continuous monitoring of the flow over as long a period as possible.

A preliminary estimate of river flows (particularly flood level and dry season levels) can be made by questioning local inhabitants but their answers should be treated with great caution. A decision on what flow rate to choose for the choice of turbine will depend on various factors such as the load pattern.

A guide to methods of measuring head and flow rate is given at Appendix III.

Figure 3 is a flow duration curve showing the design flow chosen for a particular site predicted over the year. Choice of turbine size will depend on the efficiency of the turbine at low flow rate and the marginal cost of sizing the plant for power that can only be generated over part of the year.

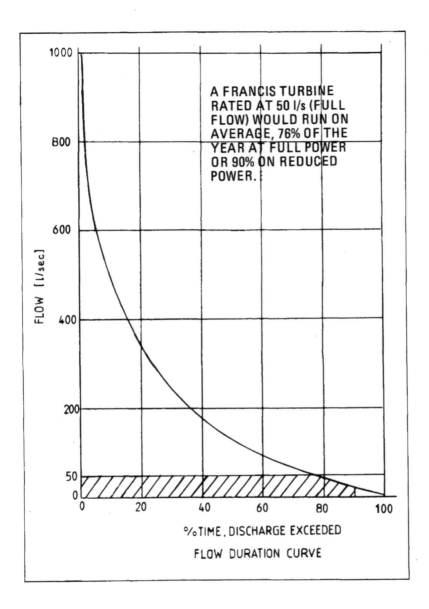

FIGURE 3

7

CIVIL WORK

Only very rarely will it be worth while constructing a dam for water storage, although a dam installed for another purpose, water supply or irrigation, could be a good place to install a turbine. However, normally they will be 'run-of-river' schemes, i.e. where the water is diverted from a river to a power channel, run down through a penstock into the turbine and then back into the river.

The choice of where to divert the river will depend on many factors: the cost of civil works, the cost of pipework, the terrain (whether rocky, subject to landslides etc) and where the power is required.

The watchword recommended by one small hydro contractor is 'The Cheapest Power, Where You Want It'. Bearing this in mind will help to decide what type of plant is to be installed, and where.

The penstock should always be as short and steep as possible, and over-, rather than under-sized (to reduce the velocity and thus the wear in the pipes and the head loss due to friction). A guide to working out the head loss in various diameter pipes is shown at Appendix IV. The head loss at full flow in some long penstocks can be as high as 30% but generally the marginal cost of the extra power that can be generated makes it worth paying for larger pipes to reduce this to around 5%.

The head race canal or leat will need a settling tank to remove large stones and heavy silt just after it has left the river. The leat should be constructed cheaply, preferably with earth banks, and the water velocity kept low to minimise erosion. At the end of the canal will be a de-silting chamber to remove remaining suspended matter, and a trash rack to remove branches, leaves and other debris, a sluice gate before the entry to the penstock and a spillway to take all excess water in the canal.

The penstock will generally be an expensive item - steel, concrete, plastic or even wooden pipe to conduct the water from the forebay to the turbine. The penstock should be well anchored at each end, supported firmly along its length and

8

preferably anchored firmly to the turbine base. Its pressure rating should be around 30% over the static head to allow for pressure surges. (More if flow control governing is used.)

The turbine and generator will be housed in a 'power house' with the turbine and generator control gear. The siting of the power house will depend on flood levels and on where the power is required. Sometimes it is preferable to use all or some of the power simply as direct mechanical shaft drive from the turbine rather than using electricity. For decentralized plants up to 100kW it is best to avoid high voltage distribution if possible so the generator should ideally be within 1 or 2 km of the load, because of the cost of transformers.

TURBINES

Turbines are divided broadly into three groups: high, medium and low head, and into two categories: impulse and reaction turbines.

	HIGH	MEDIUM	LOW
IMPULSE	PELTON TURGO	CROSS-FLOW (MITCHELL- BANKI)	
REACTION		FRANCIS	PROPELLER

The difference between impulse and reaction can be explained by saying that the impulse turbine converts the **kinetic** energy of a jet of water **in air** into movement of the turbine buckets or blades that it strikes. The blades of a reaction turbine are totally immersed in the flow of water, and the angular as well as linear momentum of the water is converted into shaft power. The pressure of water leaving the runner is reduced to atmospheric or lower. There are many types of turbine, but the types most commonly available are listed below:

Pelton Wheel (Impulse) High Head (see Fig.4)

One or more fine jets of water from fixed nozzles strike the buckets, which deflect the flow and reverse it so that, ideally the absolute velocity of the jet is reduced to zero and the water falls away with all its kinetic energy removed. The efficiency is a maximum when the speed of the bucket is half that of the jet. Because they work on high heads, pelton wheels have a high power-to-weight ratio. The buckets are a complex shape and their manufacture normally requires skilled casting, from bronze, steel or even aluminium (for very small powers). However, the casing shape is not critical and a steel or concrete box shape can be made very simply.

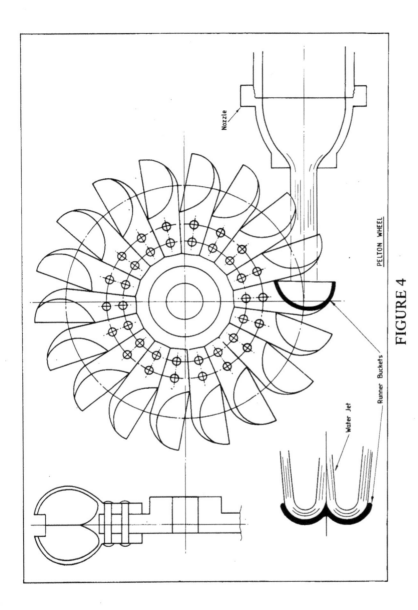

Nozzle

Water Jet

Runner Buckets

PELTON WHEEL

FIGURE 4

11

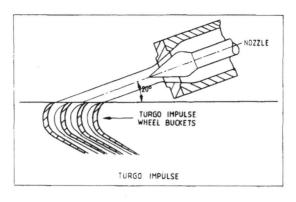

FIG. 5

Turgo Wheel (Impulse) Medium to High Head (see Fig. 5)

The turgo wheel is similar to a pelton wheel except that the jet is not in the same plane as the wheel, i.e. the water strikes the buckets and passes through the wheel. They are made in Europe by Gilbert Gilkes and Gordon of Kendal, Cumbria, U.K. They are also made in the Peoples' Republic of China.

Mitchell-Banki or Crossflow Turbine   (Impulse) Medium Head (Fig. 6)

These turbines are manufactured commercially in Europe by Ossberger A.G. of West Germany and by Armfield Engineering in the UK. The design dates from about 1910. A number of small companies manufacture this type of turbine elsewhere, for example in Nepal, Zambia, Thailand, Ireland, Pakistan and the USA. The crossflow turbine has a number of advantages. While heavier and more complex than a pelton wheel it can operate over a wide range of heads and its efficiency stays reasonably constant over a wide range of flow rates. Further, it can be manufactured in one or more standard diameters, with the width being varied to suit different sites with different power potential.

12

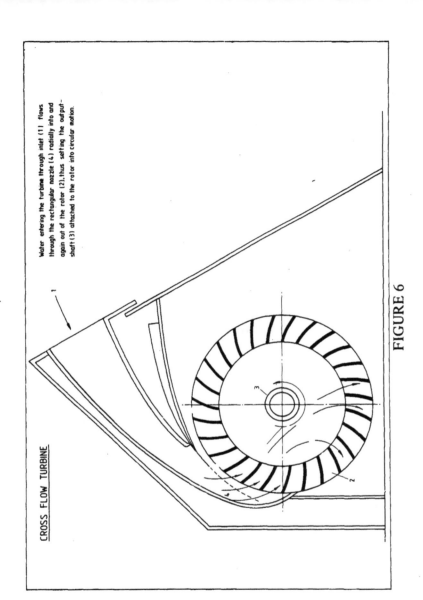

CROSS FLOW TURBINE

Water entering the turbine through inlet (1) flows through the rectangular nozzle (4) radially into and again out of the rotor (2), thus setting the output-shaft (3) attached to the rotor into circular motion.

FIGURE 6

13

It is normally considered an impulse turbine because there is air inside the casing. The jet of water strikes the blades above the rotor axis, then passes through the rotor and strikes the blades below the axis on exit, imparting angular momentum on each occasion.

Francis Turbine (Reaction) Medium Head (Fig. 7)

The water enters from around the periphery of the runner (normally via a spiral casing), passes through the guide-vanes and runner blades and exits axially from the centre.

The Francis Turbine is widely used for large hydro sites. However, for small-scale manufacture the complex patterns required for casting these turbines will often make their manufacture too expensive, particularly where a range of sizes is needed (although it is possible to fabricate the casing and runner it is a very complex technique). It should be noted, however, that in China where very large numbers of turbines are manufactured, Francis turbines are made in a range of small sizes. A number of people have demonstrated that centrifugal or mixed-flow pumps can be converted into Francis-type turbines at a much lower cost than the real article, because of the benefits of mass production. The efficiency of the pump turbine falls off rapidly as the flow rate reduces, and at 50% flow no power is delivered at all, but provided the water flow can be guaranteed when the power is needed, the saving in capital cost may be worth while. One method is to use more than one pump-turbine set to drive the alternator. At low flow rates the number of sets in use can be reduced. In many cases reducing capital cost is more important than improving the efficiency.

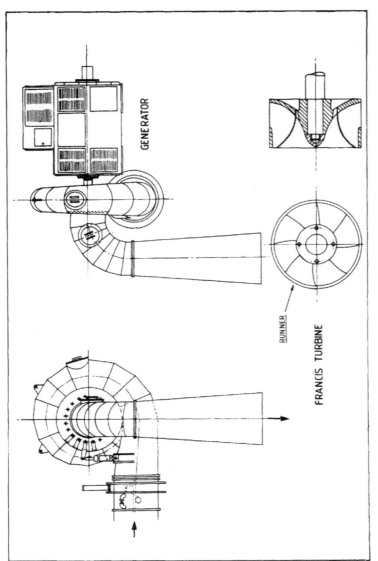

GENERATOR

RUNNER

FRANCIS TURBINE

FIGURE 7

15

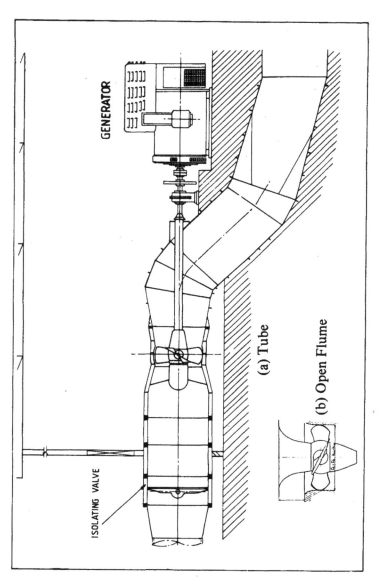

GENERATOR

ISOLATING VALVE

(a) Tube

(b) Open Flume

FIGURE 8   PROPELLER TURBINE

16

Propeller Turbines (Reaction) — Low Head (Fig. 8)

For low heads propeller turbines have the advantage of simplicity of construction. Consisting of a rotor and casing, the latter with either guide-vanes or spiral casing, they can be manufactured using casting and/or fabrication techniques. In fact the machine can be designed to be made with the very minimum of machining and the casing shape can be cast in concrete if required. The pitch of the propeller blades can be adjusted for large changes in head and flow rates. The later development of the propeller turbine — the Kaplan turbine — has controllable pitch blades and/or guide-vanes and is complicated to build. For micro-turbines this arrangement is unacceptably expensive.

Propeller turbines are broadly either 'open flume' (see fig.8) or 'tube' turbines, and there are various options for the drive arrangement. The alternator can be submerged at the hub of the turbine (bulb turbine) or even constructed around the rim of the casing ('straflo' turbine). These two methods tend to be expensive and more suited to higher powers although some cheap bulb turbines are available and can have the advantage of being immune to flooding. A more normal method for very small turbines is to have a drive shaft coming out through seals and driving the alternator by belt and pulleys to give the required speed. Gearboxes are best avoided for very small machines because of cost and maintenance problems.

ELECTRICAL

Generators

For plants up to 1.5kW it may be desirable to use d.c. generators (or a.c. with rectification as for a vehicle electrical system). Voltages can be 12 or 24 volts for battery charging or 120/220 volts for lighting etc. The advantages of using d.c. at these low power levels are that speed control is not critical, and that the low voltages are acceptable because the power does not need to be transmitted any distance and that battery storage is easily accommodated. A.C. power can be produced from the d.c solid state invertors, but invertors tend to be expensive.

The disadvantages of d.c. are unreliable brush gear and, at higher voltages, a more dangerous system.

For larger power outputs a.c. generators (alternators) are used. Single phase up to 10 to 20 kW and three phase for higher powers. Three phase alternators are cheaper per kilowatt than single phase and the transmission of three phase saves 25% of conductor costs compared with single phase. Three phase motors are also considerably cheaper than single phase and single phase motors are only commonly available up to about 7 h.p. However for community domestic distribution three phase power distributed as three separate line-to-neutral phases can be a problem. It is difficult to ensure that the three lines are even roughly equally loaded. If they are not, there will be a large current on the neutral line which will cause excessive voltage drops. So for very small community domestic installations single phase is generally to be preferred (up to at least 20kW).

For decentralized micro hydro plants it is normal to use synchronous generators, normally four pole machines to run at 1,500 rpm (50Hz) or 1,800 rpm (60Hz). Lower speed machines, with more poles, are sometimes available but will be more expensive.

These small synchronous generators are usually stand-alone units. They can be run in parallel with each other or with the grid, but they must be correctly chosen for this type

of operation and have to have additional synchronising equipment. Automatic synchronising is expensive and manual synchronising requires some skill. A cheaper and simpler solution for parallel operation with the grid is to use induction generators, which are simply normal induction motors run as generators. However they cannot normally be used independently of a main grid supply because of problems with voltage control, particularly with a varying load. There are methods of doing it, however and ITIS is working on the development of a simple electronic voltage controller to use with induction generators. The potential advantages are that induction motors are already manufactured in a large range of sizes in many developing countries and that lower speeds are available e.g. 750 rpm or 1000rpm, making direct drive from the turbine a possibility.

Speed Control

a.c. generation is at 50 or 60 Hz (cycles per second) and this frequency is controlled by the speed of the alternator. The speed therefore must be accurately controlled. Failure to keep the speed constant can result in damage to electrical machines being fed from the supply. The conventional method of speed governing with water turbines is to control the flow of water by mechanically moving valves or guide-vanes in accordance with the movement of a centrifugal governor. However, it is generally agreed that a more economic (and more precise) method for micro hydro plants is to use electronic load control. This allows the flow of water to remain constant while the hydraulic input power is balanced by the electronic output of the generator. This method also allows simpler and more reliable turbines to be used. See Appendix I.

Transmission and Distribution

Transmission at generator voltage of typically 415V, three phase is only economic up to 1 to 2 km. Beyond that, higher voltages are needed, requiring transformers. These can be a very expensive part of a micro hydro-electric system and costs will need to be carefully looked at to justify any more than local distribution. For the relative merits of three phase and single phase see 'Generators' above.

ECONOMICS

Comparative Systems' Economics

ITIS experience confirms that small-scale hydro-electric systems installed in rural areas can offer considerable financial benefits to the communities served, particularly where careful planning identifies income-generating end uses for the power. Although the cost effectiveness of such units in comparison with alternatives such as grid electricity or diesel sets depends upon local circumstances, indicative analysis for micro hydro units in the range of 10-30 kW suggests typical total capital costs of £500 - £1000 per kW with minimal subsequent maintenance costs. These costs can be reduced by the contribution of community labour for civil works and use of locally available materials.

Electronic load control devices allowing the units to be run unattended can also effect economies. With system lives well in excess of 20 years, unit generating costs have been found to be of the order of 0.7 - 1.4p per kWh (assuming capital is charged at 10% discount rate over 20 years) and unit costs of power usefully consumed 1.8 - 3.5p with a 40% load factor. A pre-requisite for keeping down the cost of power usefully consumed is to maintain a good load factor, i.e. to consume as much of the energy generated as possible. This means that productive, income-earning end-uses for the power must be introduced at the same time as the power plant. The importance of planning for a high load factor cannot be over-emphasized.

By contrast, grid power (which is rarely reliably supplied to rural areas) costs typically 2 - 5p per kWh when available, and is effectively subsidized by virtue of electricity corporation losses. In addition, where a new power line must be installed each kilometre costs £2 to £4000, often directly costed to the community. (Assuming capital charged at 10%

over 20 years), the annual capital cost per km is £240-£480, For a community, 10 kms from the grid, for instance, this would add £2400-£4800 to annual costs, equivalent to a further 1.4 - 2.8 p/kWh, assuming power demand of 20kW year-round. For a more detailed comparison with grid and diesel costs see Appendix II.

OWNERSHIP AND MANAGEMENT

When community micro hydro schemes are planned, it is important to identify clearly community-perceived needs to maximize the benefit of and mobilize fullest support for the installation. The precise management structure will depend on local preferences and experience with such institutional alternatives as ownership by:

> private individual or company
> collective/co-operative
> government department
> public corporation
> private voluntary organization

The precise management functions embrace three distinct phases in the system's life — planning, implementation, operation and in-service support.

Specific activities which give rise to the need for clear definition of responsibilities can be considered as follows:

Planning

Planning (of end uses)
Surveys (topographical, hydrological, socio-economic)
System design
Costings and Financing

Implementation

Materials requisitioning
Turbine manufacture
Civil Work Construction
Hardware Installation (including electrical distribution)

Operation and In-Service Support

Training
Operation
Tariff
Collection
Maintenance

LEGAL ASPECTS

The rights to use water to generate power often require legal definition and in some countries licences are needed to produce and sell electricity. In certain Asian countries it is even necessary to obtain a licence to conduct a survey. Potential conflicts over the use of water for power as opposed to irrigation should be carefully investigated.

MAINTENANCE

The systems should be designed for minimum maintenance but at least two operators need to be trained. They will have certain regular maintenance tasks:

> Checking voltage and frequency
> Adjusting water flow
> Cleaning the trash rack
> Flushing the silt trap
> Watching for over-topping of the canal banks
> Adjusting drive-belts (where fitted)

These operators should also be able to carry out first-level preventive and corrective maintenance:

> Drive-belt changes
> Bearing changes
> Changing turbine runner
> Changing generator slip-ring brushes (where applicable)
> Coping with basic electrical faults: fuse changing, resetting trips, possibly changing the circuit board in the load controller.

For major overhaul or breakdown maintenance the local operators will have to call on the assistance of the base engineers, who may well be a long distance from the site. It is therefore important to be able to send to the site a multi-disciplined engineer who can cope with any electrical, mechanical or civil work repairs necessary, without assistance.

LOCAL MANUFACTURE

Turbines can be made where steel fabrication, machining and possibly casting facilities are available. A decision on whether or not to manufacture locally will depend on whether sufficient sites exist to justify the dedication of valuable skill and machinery resources to this task. It will then be necessary to concentrate on one type of turbine, depending on the nature of the sites available. We recommend choosing from propeller turbines for low head, cross-flow turbines and turgo wheels for medium heads and pelton wheels for high heads. In each case it is possible to simplify the design to avoid the use of expensive machine tools or high cost materials.

It is possible to considerably reduce the cost of a turbine by, for example, casting the casing shape in concrete. A manual giving instructions for this type of technique will be available shortly from ITDG. Figure 9 shows a simply-constructed 2-jet pelton wheel of a design that will be produced in Sri Lanka.

It has proved advisable in a number of cases to use high quality bearings even for low cost small turbines because bearing failure can be catastrophic in remote sites.

It is possible to use some types of pumps as turbines but with restricted application — see 'Francis Turbines' above.

Various small companies in Europe and the USA offer small turbines at reasonable prices. A list is available from ITDG.

FIGURE 9. Two Jet Pelton Wheel

SUMMARY

Below are listed typical stages for a community micro hydro project.

1. Identify potential industrial demand for power.
2. Look for possible hydro power sites near to the industrial load centre.
3. Identify domestic electrical demand in vicinity of industrial load centre and/or power house site.
4. Size and cost the micro hydro option (civil work, mechanical and electrical costs).
5. Find local sources of hardware.
6. Cost alternative power sources (mains electricity, diesel generator set etc.)
7. Define ownership and structure for management for procurement, installation and operation.
8. Carry out detailed hydrological survey, topographical survey, system design.
9. Check legal constraints on the use of water, selling electricity etc.
10. Raise finance.
11. Construct civil work, procure and install hardware
12. Draw up tariff structure.
13. Carry out training for operation and maintenance.

Assistance with carrying out feasibility studies, site surveys, hardware procurement, installation and commissioning can be obtained from ITDG on a commercial basis. Advice on technical or managerial matters or on possible sources of finance will be given free. Write for further information to: –

ITDG, 9 King Street, London WC2E 8HN, UK or
ITIS, Myson House, Railway Terrace, Rugby CV21 3HT, UK
Telex: 311208 Myson Telephone No: 0788 - 70126.

APPENDIX I
ELECTRONIC LOAD CONTROLLER FOR WATER TURBINES

A water turbine, like most generator prime movers, requires a governing system so that a change in load (varying electrical demand) does not result in a change in speed and thus a change in the supply frequency. The usual governing method for large water turbines is a mechanical governor which regulates the flow of water through the turbine. For small hydro plants such a system is expensive, because it requires a large number of machined components, and is unnecessarily complex and difficult to maintain. A new electronic load controller, available through ITDG, governs the turbine speed by adjusting the electrical load on the alternator. (See Figure 10). As lights and electrical appliances are turned on and off the electronic controller varies the amount of power that is fed into a 'ballast' load. When there is no power being consumed on the main circuit all the output of the generator will be fed to the ballast. If main circuit power reaches the full output of the plant then no power is fed to the ballast. The adjustments are made instantaneously and even if 100 per cent of the electrical output is switched on and off at once, there will be no perceptible change in frequency. The power consumed by the ballast circuit can be used for heating, or it can be dissipated in the atmosphere. These small hydro-electric plants do not normally have dams for water storage, so there is no question of 'wasting energy'.

FIGURE 10

30

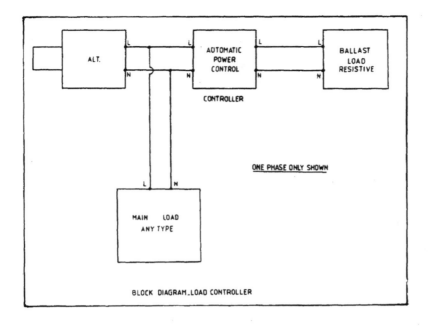

FIGURE 11

The advantages of electronic load control are:
1. The governor is cheaper and more reliable.
2. Cheaper, simpler turbines can be used with no moveable
   guide-vanes or valves.
3. Penstock pipes can be lighter and cheaper because water
   hammer is eliminated.
4. The controller can be assembled in a small workshop
   without special tools.
5. On three phase installations the load on the alternator is
   balanced.
6. The system can be easily fitted to any existing hydro-
   electric plant.

APPENDIX II: ECONOMICS OF MICRO HYDRO POWER

Cost of Grid Extension

This can be calculated using the following formula: –

$$G = U + \frac{(k.C.A)}{P}$$

Where:
G	=	total cost per kWh consumed
U	=	charge per unit (kWh) supplied by grid
k	=	length of transmission line (in kms)
C	=	unit cost per km of transmission line
A	=	annual capital charge, typically 12% (to cover depreciation and interest on capital)
P	=	power consumption (in kWh per annum)

(obviously, where no cost is incurred by a community for transmission lines, the cost per kWh of power consumed equals the unit grid charge. However, provision of the line then becomes a cost to the utility corporation, which is rarely reflected in the unit electricity charge, because few undertakings cover both operating and capital costs. This cost should be included in any analysis of power options.)

Diesel Sets

Diesel sets are rarely cost effective alternatives because they incur high maintenance and fuel costs, have short lives and pose difficulties with fuel supply. The marginal (or fuel) costs alone for generating power from diesel sets amount to 7.5p/kWh taking diesel at 33p/litre and based on fuel consumption of 4.5 litre/hour per 20kW. Fuel costs will tend to

32

account for some 75% of total diesel generating costs. The typical per kWh fuel cost for a range of diesel prices is tabulated below, based on the above specified assumptions.

Fuel Cost per kWh of Electrical Power Generated by Diesel Sets

Cost/Litre Diesel (pence)	Cost of 1 kWh power (pence)
10	2.3
20	4.5
30	6.8
40	9.0
50	11.3

In contrast to a micro hydro unit which has higher initial (capital) costs, a diesel set has lower initial costs, but higher running (fuel and maintenance) costs.

Calculation of Micro Hydro-electric System Costs

A preliminary assessment of the likely cost of electrical power can be made by using a formula which comprises three elements in the numerator — annual capital charges (to cover depreciation and interest), maintenance and labour. The formula is:

$$\text{Unit cost/kWh} = \frac{(K + M + L) \times \text{Load Factor}}{P}$$

K = annual capital charges
M = annual maintenance costs
L = annual labour costs
P = annual power generated in kWh

33

Each element is calculated as follows:

Annual Capital Charge, K

An initial micro hydro investment needs to be recovered over the anticipated life of the system at a rate which reflects the opportunity cost of capital (more commonly called the 'discount rate'). Economic analysis tends to use a system life of 20 years and discount rates of 5-10% for calculating systems economics. The table below shows the percentage of the initial investment to be charged as annual capital costs (to recover capital and earn a positive return).

Annual Capital Charge (as % of Initial Investment)

Discount Rate

Life (Years)	5%	10%	15%
10	13	16	20
15	11	13	17
20	9	12	16

Maintenance Costs, M

Maintenance and systems life are positively related and an annual allowance of 4% of initial investment costs is usually made to cover projected maintenance.

Labour Costs, L

The proportion of annual costs accounted for by labour depends on manning levels and local wage levels. However, the more successful micro hydro units have minimized direct labour costs by using electronic load control and allowing unattended operation. The emphasis is therefore on producing least-cost power, with employment creation being the objective of the end uses generated by provision of power rather than being the objective of the power plant itself.

The equation enables the use of a wide permutation of variables, depending on local circumstances, and, by addition of an element for fuel costs, can be used to compare alternatives with micro hydro units.

Load Factor

The actual unit cost of electricity consumed (as opposed to generated) depends on the system's load factor, which is a ratio of power consumption over a specified period of time to the available capacity of the generating system. In Colombia, for instance, where ITIS is (1983) funding community micro hydro units, a load factor of 40% is projected. With capital costs of £1000/kW recovered over 20 years at 10%, the unit generating cost is calculated (at present day prices) at 1.4 p/Wh. With a load factor of 40% (40% of generated power being actually usefully consumed) the unit charge per kWh becomes 3.5p/kWh. Clearly, the higher the load factor, the lower can the unit per kWh charge be set. Load factors, however, rarely exceed 50% and are dependent on the types of end use found for the power.

End Uses

ITIS' methodology for identifying viable end uses involves defining tasks/activities requiring energy (as identified by local communities) and the resource constraints acting on these. In this way, a hierarchy of end uses can be drawn up suitable for micro hydro and/or other power sources. Cost-benefit analysis is then carried out to determine the economic appropriateness of the system, paying attention to socio-economic, cultural and political constraints. For example, heat storage cookers have important implications for cooking practices. Similarly provision of piped/pumped water frees family labour for other tasks, potentially increasing a household's income-earning capacities.

Further analysis of the system's finances is also undertaken to determine the need for cash generation to cover such items as capital repayment, operating costs and maintenance and provision for spares. This determines the tariff structure and is an important consideration affecting the balance between cash-generating and time-saving end uses. Many domestic tasks involve improvements to the way of life which do not bring immediate financial benefits. Such domestic power requirements tend to be low — confined to lighting of up to 200 watts per household (although heat storage cookers of 300-400 watts offer potential for raising domestic loads). By contrast agro-processing and small-scale industrial activities are important for raising load factors. In Colombia, for instance, a load factor of 40% is projected — 10% for domestic needs, 30% for saw-milling. In Sri Lanka ITIS-supported micro hydro units established on tea estates will have an unusually high load factor of up to 75%.

A typology of end uses and likely kW loads is tabulated below:

Type	Use	kW	kWh/ton
Agro-processing	Flour grinding	1-2	40
	Oil expelling	2-3	60-90
	Crop drying		22/1% moisture
	Threshing		6-12
	Freezing		
Small Scale Industrial	Saw-milling	10-30	
	Wool and cotton processing	5-25	
	Stone crushing	5-25	
	Workshop equipment	1-10	
Household	Lighting	0.2	
	Refrigeration	0.3	
	Cooking	0.4 (heat storage cookers)	
	Water pumping	0.5-1	0.1
	(Ironing)	0.5	
	(Radio/TV)	0.1-0.3	

In summary, productive, income-generating end uses as identified above are important sources of cash, allowing surplus formation within the rural economy and enabling provisions to be made for maintenance and replacement. However, domestic end uses are also important particularly in ensuring effective community participation in system management. The balance between the two will depend on local preferences and on market opportunities for the end products.

APPENDIX III
MEASUREMENT OF HEAD AND FLOW RATE

Before the energy potential of a particular site can be calculated it is necessary to measure the range of water flows and the head through which it will fall.

1. FLOW OF WATER

The water flow will always vary widely with the seasons and in some countries by a factor of several hundred. It is therefore essential to obtain as clear a picture as possible of the flow pattern and in particular the lowest flows experienced in the dry season. (See Hydrology above). The methods described below require no special equipment and can give sufficiently accurate results if carried out carefully.

The measurements should be taken over at least one dry season and modified if necessary to allow for a particularly dry or wet measuring year.

(a) Float Timing

For this method the speed of the mid-stream surface water is measured by timing a float. Choose a part of the stream where the cross-section is regular. Measure the cross-section by finding the average depth as shown, and the width. Time the float over a short distance to obtain the speed. The average speed of the whole stream can then be calculated by multiplying the measured speed by:

0.8 for a concrete channel
0.7 for an earth channel
0.5 for a rough hill stream

For streams less than 150mm average depth, the factor becomes unpredictable and can be as low as 0.25. Overall accuracy for this method ± 80%.

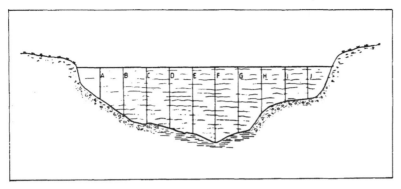

FIGURE 12

The water flow is now this corrected velocity multiplied by the cross sectional area. It is normally expressed in cubic feet per second, cubic metres per second or litres/second (1 cubic metre equals 1000 litres).

(b) Container Method

For flows up to 20 l/s, the water can be diverted into a calibrated bucket or oil drum, typically by means of a short length of plastic pipe set into a small mud dam. Several timings are then taken with a stop-watch and the average taken.

Overall accuracy for this method ± 20%.

(c) Flow over a Measuring Weir

This is usually the best method. If carried out carefully it can be very accurate (± 5%). It allows daily readings to be taken far more quickly than by any other method. Probably the easiest to construct is a rectangular wooden weir.

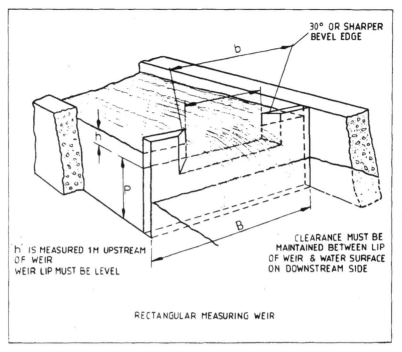

FIGURE 13

The weir must obey certain constraints. These are shown on Figs. 13 & 14. Flow is calculated from the table — Fig. 15.

The main constraints are that the weir lip width should not approach the overall weir width

$$\frac{(B - b)}{2} > 2h$$

and that the water should flow clearly off the weir lip — Fig. 3.

The height can be measured by a plastic tube immersed a distance 1 metre up-stream of the weir and with the other end placed vertically along-side the side of the weir opening with a graduated scale.

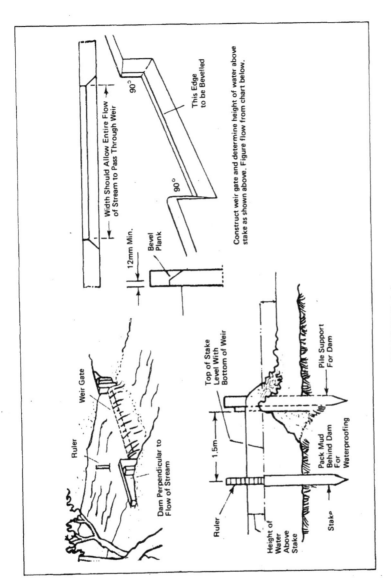

Width Should Allow Entire Flow
of Stream to Pass Through Weir

12mm Min.

Bevel
Plank

90°

90°

This Edge
to be Bevelled

Construct weir gate and determine height of water above
stake as shown above. Figure flow from chart below.

Weir Gate

Ruler

Dam Perpendicular to
Flow of Stream

Top of Stake
Level With
Bottom of Weir

1.5m

Ruler

Height of
Water
Above
Stake

Stake

Pile Support
For Dam

Pack Mud
Behind Dam
For
Waterproofing

FIGURE 14

41

Table — Flow rate for each metre width of sill

Depth (mm)	Flow Rate litres/sec
(mm)	
20	5.1
30	9.5
40	14.6
50	20.5
75	38.0
100	58.0
125	81
150	107
175	135
200	165
225	200
250	225
300	300
400	460
500	640

FIGURE 15

Weir Construction

The weir should be made from strong timber to prevent bowing under the up-stream pressure. The edges should be bevelled. On the up-stream side a polythene sheet 2m long, overlapping the weir by 0.5m on either side should be battened to the lower half.

Installation

The main practical problem is leakage under and around the weir. With muddy beds, stakes can be driven in on the down-stream face of the weir and the weir can be set into the stream bank. The weir is placed in position and the polythene stretched out on the water surface up-stream of the weir. The sheet is then sunk with rocks. With stony beds the problems are far greater. The weir will need to be roughly shaped to fit the bed. It will be difficult to drive stakes, but sandbags and rocks can be used to support and seal the weir. The upstream edge of the polythene sheet can be sealed with sand and rocks.

(d) Existing Weir Measurements

A crude estimate of flow over existing weirs and spillways can be made by measuring head and width.

The weir or spillway must be fairly level. Use Figure 13 to calculate the flow. Accuracy ± 20%.

(e) Dilution Gauging

A method which has shown to give excellent results on the most difficult sites (rocky hill streams) is dilution gauging. A known quantity of salt in solution is poured into the river and at a point further down stream the conductivity of the water is monitored with a probe and a meter. As the diluted salt solution flows past the monitoring point the conductivity of the water is recorded to give a profile of the salinity. The graph of conductivity can then be used to calculate the flow rate to an absolute accuracy of around 5%. The method is simple to use and the equipment is not expensive. Further details can be obtained from ITDG.

2. Head Measurement

The head to be measured is the difference in altitude between the penstock inlet at the forebay tank, and the turbine position. Various surveying techniques can be used.

(a) Pressure Gauge and Plastic Hose

Plastic or nylon tubing, preferably over 10m long and less than 10mm diameter is attached to a pressure gauge, preferably less than 0-4 bar (0-60 p.s.i.) range. The line is carefully bled of air, and a series of pressure readings taken (1 p.s.i. = 2.3 ft.; 1 bar = 10.2m). The pressure gauge can be checked against a known height, making this an accurate method.

(b) Spirit Level

A long straight edge e.g. a plank of wood is used with a spirit level. The assembly is rotated through 180° at each reading to reduce error.

It is essential to repeat the process two or three times to check consistency. Typical accuracy is ± 15%.

(c) Sighting with Home-made Level

A transparent tube half-filled with water can be used to sight a point further up the slope. By then going to that point and repeating the process the total head can be measured.

(d) Altimeter

A surveying altimeter, used singly, is subject to errors due to changes in atmospheric pressure with time.

Typical drifts are about 1m/minute, so for sites with difficult access the error can be considerable. It can be reduced by repeated readings, or by using two altimeters and reading both at a specified time. The latter method should give ± 1m with care.

(e) Builder's Level

Quite expensive but accurate to within a few centimetres and can give distance measurements also.

APPENDIX IV
HEAD LOSS IN PIPES

Sizeing Pipelines

To establish the head loss in a given pipeline, the following data is needed:—

— flowrate(s)
— internal pipe diameter
— pipe length
— roughness factor of pipe material
— number of and shape of bends

In practice the most critical values are the internal pipe diameter (a fourth law relationship), the flowrate (square law), and the roughness factor (which can vary over 100:1 range). The length has only a linear effect and bends are usually negligible.

The nomogram shown below applies to very smooth pipes such as p.v.c.

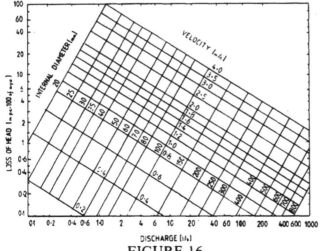

FIGURE 16
Friction loss in pipes with low friction

Old cast iron pipes should, if possible, be tested before re-use as the roughness factor is difficult to predict. Good steel pipe has generally twice the losses of p.v.c. pipe and losses in asbestos, concrete and cast iron are higher still.

To use the nomogram, read off the loss of head corresponding to the diameter and flow in question. This loss of head is then multiplied by the pipe length. The length is expressed in 100m units and head loss is then in m.

www.ingramcontent.com/pod-product-compliance
Lightning Source LLC
Jackson TN
JSHW061344131224
75386JS00052B/1804